St. Paul's Cathedral

LONDON WALL

Monument

Tower of
London

Bank of England

STREET

Tower Hill

Thames

BLACKFRIARS BRIDGE

MILLENNIUM BRIDGE

SOUTHWARK BRIDGE

CANNON STREET BRIDGE

LONDON BRIDGE

TOWER
PIER

TOWER BRIDGE

SOUTHWARK STREET

BLACKFRIARS ROAD

WATERLOO ROAD

First U.S. edition 2011

Library of Congress Cataloging-in-Publication Data
Rubbino, Salvatore, date.
A walk in London / Salvatore Rubbino.
p. cm.
ISBN 978-0-7636-5272-2
1. London (England)—Juvenile literature. 2. London (England)—History—Juvenile literature. 3. Walking—England—London—Juvenile literature. I. Title.
DA677.R83 2011
942.1—dc22   2010038769

11 12 13 14 15 16 17 LEO 10 9 8 7 6 5 4 3 2 1

Printed in Heshan, Guangdong, China

This book was typeset in MKlang Bold and Futura Book.
The illustrations were done in mixed media.

Candlewick Press
99 Dover Street
Somerville, Massachusetts 02144

visit us at www.candlewick.com

**For my beautiful boys,
Billy and Tom**

A WALK in LONDON

Salvatore Rubbino

CANDLEWICK PRESS

Most people call the clock tower of the Palace of Westminster "Big Ben," but in fact Big Ben is the name of the bell inside the clock.

The clock has been ticking since 1859. It keeps very good time.

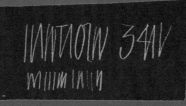

London is the capital city of the United Kingdom. It has around 7.5 million citizens.

Double-decker buses have been riding London's streets since the 1930s.

Hello! There's **me**, and that's my mom! We just got off the bus in Westminster—in the heart of central **London!**

A tall clock strikes. "That's **Big Ben**," Mom tells me. "It's eleven o'clock. Good, we're just in time!"

St. James's Park is a royal park and lies between three palaces: the Palace of Westminster, Buckingham Palace, and St. James's Palace.

"In time for what?" I want to know.
"Wait and see!" Mom says.
"This way—through St. James's Park."
The park is full of water,
and the water's full of birds.
So are the benches. . . .

More than 1,000 trees grow in St. James's Park.

"Hello!" I say.
"That's a pelican," Mom says.
"It's very rare to meet one."

The first pelicans to live in St. James's Park were given to King Charles II in 1664 by the Russian ambassador.

"Here we are!" Mom says. We've reached the **biggest** house I've ever seen!

"Buckingham Palace is where the royal family lives," Mom tells me. "Every day, new sentries come to guard it, and there's a ceremony called the Changing of the Guard."

Behind the fence, a fancy black car is waiting. "I think the royal family is going for a drive!" I say.

A flag always flies above the palace. There are two flags: one for when the monarch's away, and this one, for when the monarch's in London.

Buckingham Palace has its own post office and its own postcode: SW1A 1AA.

Buckingham Palace has 775 rooms, including the Throne Room, the Music Room, the Marble Hall, the Picture Gallery, the Yellow Drawing Room, the Chinese Luncheon Room, and the Ballroom.

The Changing of the Guard takes place at 11:30 sharp every morning in spring and summer, and every other morning in fall and winter.

During the ceremony, the New Guard receives the Palace keys from the Old Guard while a full military band plays.

Not many people know that London's official central point is on
a rotary just south of Trafalgar Square.

After the ceremony, Mom takes me to a special place to stand.
"Now you're standing at the very center
of the center of London!" she tells me.

We listen to a visitor reading from his guide book:

"From this spot, Manchester is 184 miles away, Rome is 1,118 miles away,
Sydney is 10,500 miles away, and the moon is about 240,000 miles away."

"And look, TRAFALGAR SQUARE is just
thirty feet away!" Mom says, laughing.

Admiral Nelson died at sea at the battle of Trafalgar in 1805. This column with his statue at the top stands 169 feet high.

Four lions lie at the statue's base to guard it. They are made out of bronze, which is kept shiny by all the visitors who come to sit on them.

Every winter since 1947, Norway has sent Londoners a very tall Christmas tree. It always stands in Trafalgar Square.

We cross the traffic, and I start to run. There are fountains and some lions I want to sit on!

I'm really hungry! Mom takes me to a café where you can sit outside to eat. We ask for fish and chips.

"This is COVENT GARDEN PIAZZA," Mom says. "No cars allowed!"

Instead the road is full of acrobats and jugglers.

Street entertainers are allowed to perform in Covent Garden every day except Christmas Day.

Few roads in London are closed to traffic but Covent Garden Piazza is one of them.

Until 1974, London's biggest fruit-and-flower market was held here every day.

I put some money in the hat of someone standing upside down!

Fish and chips is one of the most popular meals in Britain. About 300 million servings are eaten each year.

THEATRE ROYAL DRURY LANE

NEW MUSICAL

London is Europe's third rainiest city. About twenty-three inches of rain falls here every year.

Oh, dear! It's raining! Some people have umbrellas, but some — like us — forgot!

The streets turn shiny. We cross one to a store that sells exactly what we need!

FOOD & NEWS
29

WE SELL UMBRELLAS

Queen's Head

A London telephone booth is a good place to wait out a shower.

West of the dragon, the road is called the Strand.

East of the dragon, it's called Fleet Street.

It's nice and dry under our new umbrella. I look around as we walk. "Careful, there's a dragon!" I warn Mom.

"So far we've been walking in Westminster," Mom says, "but if we step beyond the statue, we'll be in the oldest part of London . . .

The emblem of the City is a dragon because in myths, dragons guard treasure, and the City is where most of London's banks are.

The City boundary is called Temple Bar.

18

Ye Olde Cheshire Cheese

'the City.' The City's full of history."

It's full of sunshine too! The rain has gone away.

The City is sometimes called the Square Mile, because that's how big it is.

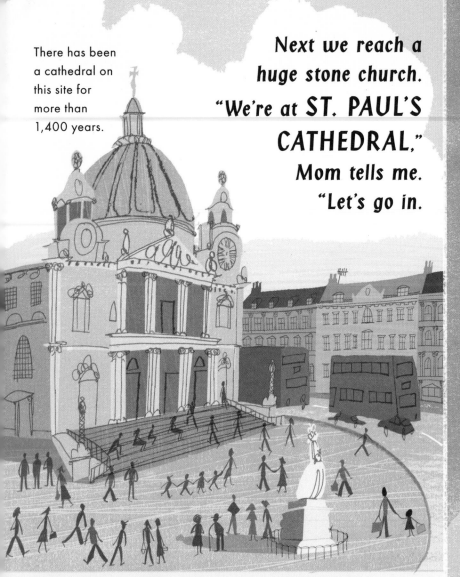

There has been a cathedral on this site for more than 1,400 years.

Next we reach a huge stone church. "We're at **ST. PAUL'S CATHEDRAL**," Mom tells me. "Let's go in.

There's a Whispering Gallery inside."
We climb around

and around

and around,
until we're in the dome.

There are 259 steps up to St. Paul's Whispering Gallery.

A whisper against the wall on one side of the dome can be heard 105 feet away on the other.

The cathedral's dome weighs about 64,000 tons.

Three St. Paul's Cathedrals
have burned to the ground.
The current one was designed
by Christopher Wren.

Mom and I stand
in different places, then
she whispers "Hello?" I jump!
It sounds as if she's right
beside me.

The streets near the cathedral have interesting names:
Bread Street, Ironmonger Lane — this one's called
THREADNEEDLE STREET.

"There's the Bank of England,"
Mom says. "Britain's oldest bank."

Around the corner, we find the bank's museum.
In the display cases, there's lots of money! Coins . . .

Modern British currency has eight coins. They have to be light enough to carry in your pocket, but strong enough to circulate for many years.

British coins used to be made of almost pure silver or gold. Now they are made of less valuable metals, like steel, nickel, and brass.

British coins are struck, or "minted," at the Royal Mint, which used to be in the Tower of London. Now it's near Cardiff, in Wales.

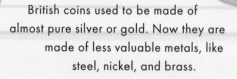

The Bank of England was founded in 1694 as a place for people to store their gold safely. In return, the bank gave them paper receipts, like this one.

Today the bank prints just four banknotes—£5, £10, £20, and £50—on watermarked paper. It is very hard to counterfeit the notes, but criminals try all the time.

paper money . . .

and even a bar of gold!

Ooooooof!

I try to lift it, but I'm not strong enough.

Underground, the Bank still stores thousands of bars of pure 24-carat gold in vaults. Each bar is worth more than $300,000 and weighs about 29 pounds.

You can climb the 311 spiral steps inside the Monument to see the view from the top. When you come down again, you will be given a certificate!

Christopher Wren designed the Monument to stand 202 feet high because it is 202 feet east of the bakery in Pudding Lane where the Great Fire started.

The column is built out of 28,196 cubic feet of Portland stone.

We're tired now, so we find a bench and sit down near a tall stone column. "That's called THE MONUMENT," Mom says. "It was built in memory of the Great Fire of London, See the bowl of copper flames on top?"

"I like history stories," I tell Mom. "Then there's one more thing to show you," she says.

The Great Fire of London broke out on September 2, 1666, and lasted for four days, burning thousands of city streets and buildings.

The world's first underground trains ran beneath the river in London. The trains had no windows, and passengers found the ride very rough.

UNDERGROUND

MONUMENT STATION

SUNNY SPELLS NEXT WEEK

WOW! A real castle
in the middle of the city!

"Nowadays, kings and queens live
at Buckingham Palace," Mom tells
me, "but long ago they
lived here, at the
TOWER OF LONDON."

As well as
being a palace,
the Tower was
a prison. Famous
inmates included
Guy Fawkes,
Anne Boleyn, and
Sir Walter Raleigh.

JEWEL
HOUSE

We buy tickets and join a guided
tour with a soldier
called a Beefeater.

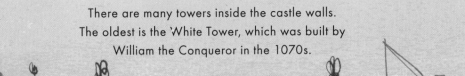

There are many towers inside the castle walls.
The oldest is the 'White Tower, which was built by
William the Conqueror in the 1070s.

WHITE
TOWER

Seven ravens live at the Tower. The Ravenmaster
feeds them 170 grams of raw meat every day, an
egg a week, and occasionally a rabbit.

BLOODY TOWER

TRAITORS'
GATE

The Tower's outer walls are about
50 feet high and 45 feet thick.

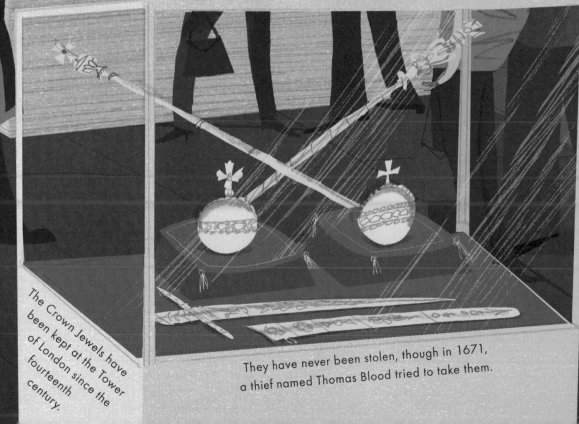

"**This way!**" calls our guide.
And suddenly it's really dark!

We've come inside the *Jewel House*,
where the only things that shine are royal
swords and cups and scepters.

The Crown Jewels have been kept at the Tower of London since the fourteenth century.

They have never been stolen, though in 1671, a thief named Thomas Blood tried to take them.

"What makes the crown so sparkly?" I whisper.
"Diamonds!" a boy in our group whispers back.

The Imperial State Crown has 2,868 diamonds, 17 sapphires, 11 emeralds, 5 rubies, and 273 pearls in it.

The monarch wears it every year at the State Opening of Parliament.

Until 1749, there was only one bridge across the Thames in London. Now there are many ways to get across, including road bridges, footbridges, rail bridges, and tunnels beneath the riverbed.

More planes fly over London than over any other city in the world.

More people live in London than in any other city in the European Union.

More than 300 different languages are spoken here.

London is about 20 centuries old. The first Romans to settle here came in AD 43.

The London Eye lifts 3.5 million visitors a year 443 feet high above the city. On a clear day you can see for 25 miles in any direction.

The Palace of Westminster is where members of Parliament debate new laws to govern the country. You can visit the public gallery to watch them doing it for free.

The Thames in London is tidal, so its water is partly fresh and partly salt. It is home to lots of fish, including trout, bass, and flounder.

When Londoners talk about "North London" and "South London," they mean north and south of the river.

Outside the Tower, there are boats!
"Here's London's famous river," Mom says. "The Thames."
"Ferry to Westminster!"
shouts a boatman on the pier.
"Let's take it back to where we started," says Mom.
And the next thing I know,
we're out on the water with the wind!

The River Thames is 210 miles long, and flows west-east from Gloucestershire to the North Sea.

Although the North Sea is forty-two miles away, you often see seagulls in London.

Londoners often give new buildings on their skyline nicknames:

this one is known as the Gherkin. Its real name is 30 St. Mary Axe.

Between the fourteenth and nineteenth centuries, winters were so cold that the river often froze. Londoners could skate or sled across it, and frost fairs were held on the ice.

comes
amesa,"
ark

Altogether, London covers an area of about 660 square miles. It is divided into thirty-two districts, or "boroughs."

Completed in 1710, St. Paul's Cathedral was the city's tallest building for two and a half centuries.

In 1968, the previous London Bridge was sold to an American, who rebuilt it in Arizona.

TATE MODERN, BANKSIDE

SHAKESPEARE'S GLOBE

The word *Thames* from the Celtic "T which means or muddy.

Back on land, we wait for our bus home.
My legs feel wobbly!

Big Ben strikes.
"Six o'clock,"
Mom counts.
"Just in time," I say.
"For what?" Mom asks.
"To see the royal family!"
I say, waving at the
fancy black car
that's going by.

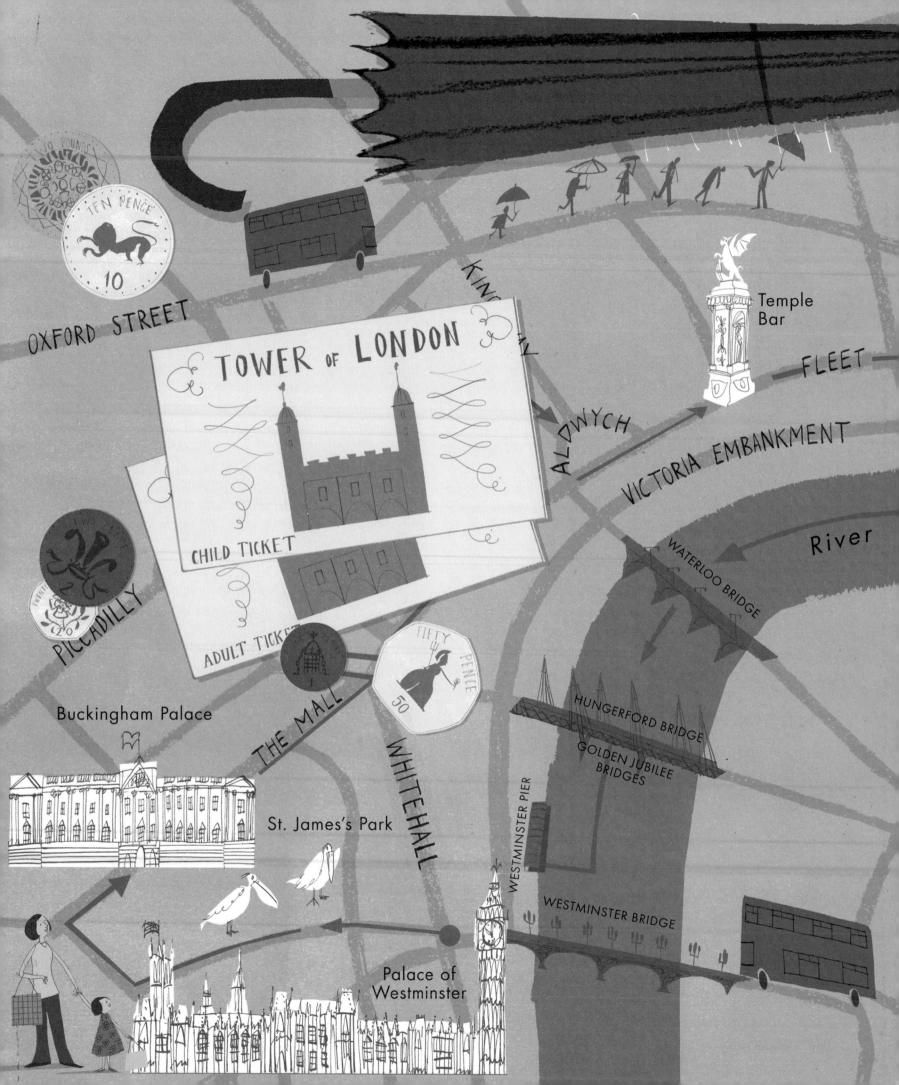